48 years a mother
68 years a Montanan!
Happy Mother's Day
May 11, 1975
Bob, Margaret, Mary Ellen
Mark & Kathy

FATHER RAVALLI'S MISSIONS

Father Anthony Ravalli, S.J. (1812–1884). Montana Historical Society.

FATHER RAVALLI'S MISSIONS

HAROLD ALLEN

THE GoodLion

THE SCHOOL OF THE ART INSTITUTE OF CHICAGO

CHICAGO ILLINOIS USA

ISBN 0–912844–03–5

Michigan & Adams Street / Chicago / Illinois 60603

First Printing, January 1972

A mi esposa María

Cross, made of diseased pine by Father Ravalli. About two feet high.
Montana Historical Society. H. A.

FOREWORD

One of many affecting incidents related about Father Anthony Ravalli, the pioneer-architect-sculptor-craftsman-physician-priest, tells of a time when he was nearing the end of his forty years as a Jesuit missionary in the Northwest. A friend asked if he had never wanted to return to Italy to see again his native land and his friends and family. "Yes," he replied, "and I could have had that pleasure. But then the sacrifice would not have been complete." And, bowing his head, he wept like a child.

Another tale recalls an event that occurred years earlier when Father Ravalli was at Colville. Hearing a report that an unhappy Indian woman had just hanged herself nearby, he rushed to the spot, cut the woman down, and, finding her still warm, started immediately to breathe into her mouth, meanwhile raising and lowering her arms. Though the Indians, watching with shocked fascination, obviously thought his actions futile and foolish, he persisted for almost an hour, when the woman finally began again to breathe for herself, opened her eyes, and eventually, before the incredulous watchers, rose and went home, where she is said to have lived to an advanced age. This triumph of knowledge, skill, patience, and humanity earned for Father Ravalli a reputation among the Indians as their greatest medicine man.

Both stories radiate the strong personal magnetism that seems to abound in everything Father Ravalli did or made. He had a rare ability to communicate. And this, even more than his undeniable talents of hand and mind, is what made him both an artist and a person to whom—almost ninety years after his death—it is hard to react but with personal involvement and affection. One senses this immediately on entering either of his churches. One feels it talking with their caretakers, who reveal an excitement that, apparently, custom cannot stale. One meets it trying to answer the questions of visitors: those who have seen his churches often, and those seeing them for the first time. One sees it on the map of Montana, where a vast and beautiful county is named Ravalli. And one can read it between the lines carved in the marble of Father Ravalli's gravestone, a monument that was paid for not by the Church but by many small contributions from people all over Montana, and far beyond.

This remarkable man, Antonio Ravalli, was born 16 May 1812 in Ferrara, Italy. He entered the Society of Jesus 12 November 1827, and, following his noviceship, studied in Jesuit colleges and in Rome. He taught in the Society's schools in Turin and Piedmont and, having completed his theological studies, was ordained a priest in 1843. Joining Father Pierre-Jean De Smet's party of missionaries, Father Ravalli made his final vows while on the voyage to America, where the party arrived in Oregon at the end of July 1844. After a winter at St. Paul's Mission on the Willamette, Father Ravalli was sent to Colville, now Washington, to build a church; but only a month later he was transferred to St. Mary's Mission among the Flathead Indians in what is now western Montana. When St. Mary's closed temporarily in 1850, Father Ravalli was sent to the Sacred Heart Mission among the Coeur d'Alene Indians, now in northern Idaho, where he designed the great church at Cataldo and made its altars and statues. From 1857 to 1860 he was at Colville again, then from 1860 to 1863 served as Master of Novices and spiritual adviser at Santa Clara College in California. Preferring the frontier, he returned in 1863, going first to St. Ignatius Mission and from there, the following year, to St. Peter's Mission—both now in Montana. Then, in 1866, he was brought back to "dear old St. Mary's," where he designed the remarkable new church, and—save for frequent excursions to serve other localities as physician and priest—there he remained till his death on 2 October 1884.

As an artist, Anthony Ravalli is never listed among the select and fascinating company of his contemporaries who depicted the early West. And the reason is clear: he did not depict the early West. He stayed in the West longer than any of that company, producing works of art, apparently, wherever he went, but, unlike Father Nicholas Point, Father Ravalli left behind no Indian portraits, no paintings of buffalo hunts. With the Italian gusto of a talented man trained in the traditional arts of Europe, Father Ravalli used them—with never a doubt that they were the best he could give—not only to brighten the world wherever he went but to transform it toward a civilized ideal. And he was right. As the Indians had been charmed and won by Father Point's paintings, they thrilled to toil on Father Ravalli's churches, and in the process became more complete men. And today we, with different eyes, look with wonder at his churches, so oddly and beautifully out of time and place, and are happier and better for the experience.

But it is not only as an artist that Father Ravalli is remembered with marvel and affection. As the wilderness changed, he served far more than as a gifted missionary to the Indians. Miners vied for the privilege of offering him hospitality when he visited their camps, because in his sermons (which everyone attended) he spoke as a strong, brave, simple man delivering an important message to strong, brave, simple men—all of whom were his close friends. Though today we tend to think of him largely as a craftsman and architect, in his own time Father Ravalli was more widely famous and revered as an accomplished and skillful physician. His hearty bedside manner alone could cure, and he was always selflessly willing to travel any distance in any weather to help a suffering Indian or white, rich or poor, without thought of recompense.

Many beholden people were deeply moved by Father Ravalli's good works and shining talents during his lifetime, but he is still remembered in the Northwest with special affection, and famous as a missionary second only to De Smet, the perpetual publisher. Perhaps this is because this "great, good man," as Father Ravalli was called in his own time, was whole to a rare degree, gifted and accomplished in all areas that enhance a man, great as a person as well as priest, artist, mechanic, and physician. He won people's hearts by the warmth of his own heart; he understood that beauty is something we all yearn for; he never made the mistake, as most of us do, of putting it in second place—and so piled up treasures in heaven and left treasures on earth too.

Even this brief description of only a part of Father Ravalli's work would not exist but for the help of many people. I owe special thanks to: Hugh Edwards, in whose History of Photography classes I first assembled these photographs; Paul Pearson, with whom I first visited and photographed both of Father Ravalli's churches; Mr. and Mrs. Raymond White and their children, the caretakers of the Cataldo Mission, and R. J. Bush, custodian of St. Mary's, each of whom has gone cheerfully out of his way to help me; Joseph P. Donnelly, S.J., Father Point's translator, who read my manuscript and suggested changes that improved it; Wilfred P. Schoenberg, S.J., archivist of the Oregon Province of the Society of Jesus, for varied, spontaneous, and prompt help, much of it beyond the line of duty; all the authors, living and dead, listed in the notes and bibliography; and the libraries and collections that furnished illustrations in the text. All this indispensable and deeply appreciated aid would have been insufficient without a generous grant from the School of the Art Institute of Chicago, which makes this book possible.

Blackfeet Indians hunting buffalo. Color lithograph from a drawing by John Mix Stanley, 1853. Reports of Explorations and Surveys . . . , *XII-1, Plate XXVII. Newberry Library.*

IN OUR increasingly cramped and tarnished world of the 1970's it is hard to realize that scarcely more than a century and a third ago the entire northwestern corner of our country was a sparkling, primeval wilderness. Save for animal and Indian trails it was trackless, though, by the 1820's, a few isolated forts had begun to supply the handful of white beaver trappers who gladly risked perpetual dangers for the unparalleled excitements and freedoms they found in the vast, enchanted land. Because both England and the burgeoning United States claimed this virgin paradise, its ultimate nationality was still uncertain. Until well into the 1840's it was wide open for whichever country could settle it first.

Since both claimants possessed the sublime, Christian confidence that condoned every nation that settled in the Western Hemisphere, the Indians who already lived here, and presumably owned the land, did not count. True, they were few compared with the human population this region now sustains, and comprised a varied lot. The coastal tribes, living on the forested shores of the ocean and its rivers, had developed a remarkable village culture, already altering because of the white man's recent arrival. On its eastern edge, where the Rocky Mountains rise, the vast, disputed region touched the Great Plains, where nomadic tribes—the Blackfeet, the Crows, the Sioux, and others—based their lifeways on hunting the still countless buffalo. These tribes, scarcely a century earlier, had experienced a sudden—and temporary—renaissance: the result of Spanish horses from Mexico, which transformed their hunting and transportation from drudgery into exciting pastimes, and produced, for a few generations, an affluence and mobility the Indians had never known on foot and were soon to lose with the buffalo.

Between these diverse tribes were others in the forested mountains. These Indians lived on game and, to an extent that made many of them independent, on abundant root plants. Because the mountain buffalo, after almost a century of horse hunting, was no longer plentiful, the mountain Indians had begun to make seasonal expeditions to the plains for buffalo meat, contesting the hunting grounds with the fierce Blackfeet and Crows. In what we now call Wyoming, Montana, Idaho, and Utah were the Shoshones, and farther north, in present western Montana, the similar Flatheads. Farther west, in Idaho and eastern Washington and Oregon, lived the Nez Perces, Coeur d'Alenes, and Cayuses. All lived largely in tepees, ranging over the green mountains and intervening deserts of the Rockies.

Most of these mountain Indians were remarkably enlightened, from the white man's point of view, and as a group were more friendly and cooperative than the hostile Plains tribes. With the exception of the Cayuses, who were apt to be backward and suspicious, they were fascinated by the white man and anxious to learn from him. The Shoshones, led during most of the nineteenth century by their wise chief, Washakie, had a reputation among both whites and Indians for honesty, hospitality, and general dependability. Though the Coeur d'Alenes, named 'heart of an awl' by French-speaking trappers, clannishly shunned whites and warred with their Indian neighbors, they sought missionaries eagerly and quickly became successful farmers. The Flatheads and Nez Perces, remarkable Indians by all reports, were clean, honest, generous, and friendly, frequently allying themselves with each other and with whites in business and war.

A Nez Perce Indian named Rabbit's Skin Leggings. Oil portrait by George Catlin, 1832. One of four men the Flatheads and Nez Perces sent to St. Louis in 1831 to get 'Black Robes' for the two tribes. National Collection of Fine Arts, Smithsonian Institution.

All the Western Indians had begun only recently to emerge from a stone-age culture, because of things the white man had brought, and were suddenly becoming increasingly dependent on him—for guns, ammunition, knives and other steel tools, cloth, glass beads, and whiskey, things they could not possibly produce themselves. To the Indian mind these wonders seemed the products of pure magic, and the Indians knew their future was dark unless they too could learn its secrets. Their religion taught them they could wrest what they wanted from nature through the magic of shamans, medicine men, who could wield supernatural powers. If only they could attract and keep one of the white man's magicians, the Flatheads and Nez Perces reasoned, they too might share all the powers and riches the white man controlled.

Contrary to early reports, still commonly believed, the Flatheads did not flatten their children's heads. 'Flathead' is merely a verbal translation of the sign language gesture for their Indian name. They were somewhat more ready for the white man's magic because, although no missionary had yet been near them, already they had been exposed to Christianity—or a rude but inspiring version of it—through Iroquois refugees they had adopted into their tribe. These roughly Catholic Iroquois, the descendants of Eastern Indians the Jesuits had converted as early as the seventeenth century, described such a convincing vision of a better life —successful battles, prodigal buffalo hunts, and the resulting power and wealth—that the inspired Flatheads and Nez Perces decided to act. And thereby they unknowingly set in motion a series of events and forces which ultimately determined that the land now Washington, Oregon, and Idaho would become part of the United States. Beyond this stupendous result, the Flathead endeavor produced several fortunate by-products which enrich the history of the Northwest, among them: Father De Smet's happy and precious writings; Father Point's word-and-picture descriptions—heartwarming, ingenuous, and beautiful—of a vanished Eden; the Flathead conversion itself, a delightful oasis in the dry history of proselyting reluctant savages; and Father Ravalli's two remarkable churches, which we examine here.

The Flathead conversion appeals irresistibly because of the eagerness—even insistence—the Indians showed in soliciting missionaries. They wanted medicine men more powerful than those their rivals had, and the Iroquois had convinced them that the 'Black Robes' (Jesuits) with their 'big prayer' (the Mass) were the answer. To get a resident Black Robe they sent a succession of embassies to the white man's distant world. Most of these efforts failed, for the way was dangerous, but one of them had the immense consequences we have already mentioned. In the spring of 1831 the Flatheads sent four men (one Flathead and three Nez Perces) to the nearest place a Jesuit might be found, St. Louis, sixteen hundred miles away across the harsh plains, teeming with their enemies. Traveling, for safety, with a white caravan, all four men reached St. Louis by fall, but two of them died there that winter (for, as always for Indians, civilization was more perilous than the trail) and were buried as Christians. The other two left in the spring of 1832, bewildered but with a vague promise of Black Robes for their tribes. They had come on horseback, following the rivers the wagon trains would soon retrace, but they returned by the other great route to the West, that of Lewis and Clark, by boat up the Missouri.

The Flathead story has almost the sound of myth, full of coincidences and timely chances. The two Indians happened to travel on the *Yellowstone*, which in 1832 was the first steamboat to ascend the Missouri through two thousand miles of wild country to Fort Union at the mouth of the Yellowstone River. Another passenger was the painter George Catlin, making his first trip to record the western Indians. When the boat paused at Fort Pierre, Catlin painted many pictures of the local Sioux, and portraits of both our Indians, dressed in finery the Sioux probably had given the two celebrities in recognition of their dangerous errand. Near the mouth of the Yellowstone one of the pair died, and

A Nez Perce Indian named No Horns on His Head. Oil portrait by George Catlin, 1832. Catlin painted the two Nez Perces in Sioux costumes while they were returning from St. Louis. National Collection of Fine Arts, Smithsonian Institution.

the survivor continued alone. Still east of the mountains he fell in with a band of hunting Nez Perces, and so was able to deliver his message. But before he could return to his friends, the dreaded Blackfeet killed him, in the fall of 1832.

Having heard of the Jesuits' promise, both Nez Perces and Flatheads came eagerly the following summer to the annual mountain rendezvous (in 1833 on the Green River) where trappers and Indians met with traders from 'the States' to barter beaver pelts for supplies, exchange news, and revel in the lonely mountain men's long deferred carousal. The Indians came hoping for Black Robes—but none was there.

Meanwhile, though, a persuasively garbled account of the Flathead embassy to St. Louis had reached the New England Protestants. Playing up the perilous but sublimely inspired journey in pathetic contrast with the mistakenly supposed practice of head-flattening, it stressed the urgency of saving these yearning heathens from the imminent clutches of Rome. Eloquent, though not completely accurate, this appeal roused a long dormant American interest in disputed 'Oregon'—and a wide and holy envy for the souls of its dusky, groping, and supposedly self-mutilated savages—flatheaded but searching for God. As a result, the Reverend Jason Lee, a Methodist, was at the rendezvous of 1834, the first of a quickening succession of Protestant missionaries to come to the mountains. He had been sent with the gospel and four assistants to answer the Flathead call, and though he was not a Black Robe, the Flatheads might have taken him anyway, so great was their need. Yet, though his Board of Foreign Missions had specifically ordained him Missionary to the Flathead Indians, Lee seems to have been strangely disappointed and repelled by what he found. Perhaps, if these Indians' heads really had been flat, as reported, he might have felt a stronger call. Instead, leaving the expectant Flatheads, he rushed on to what seemed to him a more promising labor among the already cowed Chinooks south of the Columbia (some of whom did flatten their heads). Lee hoped to make the Chinooks into Methodist farmers, and to his attempt, abetted from 'the States,' we owe the American settlement of the Willamette Valley.

Two years later, in 1836, at the Green River rendezvous the Indians found the Presbyterians Marcus Whitman and Henry Spalding—and their wives, the first white American women to cross the Continental Divide. The missions these two couples founded—the Spaldings' among the Nez Perces near what is now Lewiston, Idaho, and the Whitmans' among the treacherous Cayuses, somewhat east of Fort Walla Walla—were precious American outposts. Because of its location the Whitman Mission became a valued stop on the early Oregon Trail, which, within a decade, would flood the Oregon Country with Americans—and make it American. Narcissa Whitman's daughter, born in the spring of 1837, was the first all-white American child born in that contested land. In the winter of 1842 Marcus Whitman made a deservedly well publicized horseback trip to Boston and Washington, asking for settlers and government protection, and the following summer guided successfully to Oregon the first large caravan of Americans: about a thousand people. Even the Cayuse massacre of the Whitmans in 1847, a year after England had agreed by treaty to American sovereignty south of the forty-ninth parallel, seemed to further the 'Oregon' cause. For the famous mountain man Joe Meek (whose half-breed daughter was one of the victims) rode east to make a personal report to the President of the United States (who happened to be his cousin), demanding American protection for its pioneer citizens. Meek's appeal roused further interest in the West and probably did not hinder James K. Polk in his continuing attempt to get Congress, absorbed in the problems of slavery and the Mexican War, to act strongly on the Oregon question. Congress made Oregon a territory in 1848.

These events might have happened anyway. But it is clear that they happened when they did because the Flatheads sent for help.

Still, all through the 1830's the Flatheads lacked a Black Robe. In 1835 a three-man embassy rode to St. Louis again, and again received a promise. Another attempt, in 1837, ended when the Sioux massacred all five Indian delegates on the North Platte. Finally, in 1839, two more men made the long trip, this time by canoe down the Yellowstone and Missouri Rivers. At Council Bluffs they met the Jesuit Father Peter J. De Smet, then working to convert and civilize the Potawatomi Indians. He advised the messengers to continue to St. Louis and appeal to Bishop Rosati. There they received a promise so definite that, while one remained to guide the Black Robe, the other returned with the good news.

The Black Robe chosen was Father De Smet. He was eager as he rode up the Platte with the American Fur Company caravan, and his Indian companion, in the spring of 1840—toward the last rendezvous. There would be no more, for silk had replaced fur for hats, and beaver depletion and competing fur companies had taken the profits out of trapping. It is symbolic that Father De Smet's journey, the vanguard of Catholic missionary effort in the mountains, should have coincided with the final endeavor of the dying fur trade. Lewis and Clark had first penetrated this mysterious wilderness in 1805. Then for a full generation, while settlers hesitated before its awful barriers, the mountain men had visited every cranny of the waiting land. Now that the time of trapping was past, the country was at least explored for the permanent population which would soon follow the missionaries. Father De Smet rode west past the great, unforgettable landmarks of the imminent Oregon Trail (Chimney Rock, Independence Rock, Devil's Gate), and then at the rendezvous on Green River celebrated, with deep emotion,

Lithograph from a drawing by Father Nicholas Point, S.J., 1846. De Smet, Oregon Missions, *opposite page 297. Newberry Library.*

the first Mass west of the Divide. Here too he met the ten Flathead warriors who had come to escort him to their tribe, waiting eagerly in Pierre's Hole at the headwaters of Henry's Fork of the Snake in northeastern Idaho. United there, the whole party moved like a pilgrimage, northward across the Continental Divide again and into the Flathead homeland.

After only a month among the Flatheads Father De Smet left for reinforcements, but returned the next spring (1841) —ten years after the first Flathead delegation reached St. Louis. He brought twelve other men, among them Father Nicholas Point, the French priest whose 'recollections' and wonderful, naive paintings of the Indians were only recently revealed in a beautiful book, *Wilderness Kingdom*, one of the publishing events of 1967. Choosing a mission site in the Bitterroot Valley, the Black Robes named the mission, the river, and the mountain peak in the Bitterroot Range to the west "St. Mary's."

Immediately they laid out a plan for the projected village, divided the land, and planned the various structures, those needed first being a church, a school, workhouses, and storehouses. It was already fall, and construction had to begin at once on buildings that would serve temporarily as a church and residences, and later as farm dependencies. Father De Smet describes how

> the Flatheads assisting us with their whole heart and strength, had in a short time, cut from 2,000 to 3,000 stakes, and the three Brothers, with no other tools than an axe, saw and auger, constructed a chapel with pediment, colonnade and gallery, balustrade, choir, seats, etc., by St. Martin's day. . . .

That was 11 November. On 2 December,

> the Fathers . . . assembled the people, and great was their astonishment on beholding the decorations of the chapel.

> Some days previously the Fathers had engaged all who were willing, to make mats of rushes or straws. All the women, girls and children assembled eagerly for this good work, so that they had enough to cover the floor and ceiling and hang around the walls. The mats, ornamented with festoons of green, made a pretty drapery around the altar. On a canopy was inscribed the holy name of Jesus. Among the ornaments they placed a picture of the Blessed Virgin over the tabernacle; on the floor of the tabernacle a representation of the heart of Jesus. The pictures of the way of the cross, in red frames, the lights, the silence of night . . . so well disposed the minds and hearts of our Indians, that it would have been scarcely possible to find on earth an assembly of savages more resembling a company of saints.[1]

Father Point's view of the interior in *Oregon Missions* remarkably echoes Father De Smet's description.

Late in December most of the Indians, accompanied by Father Point, left for the great buffalo hunt, but construction continued in "erecting around our establishment a strong palisade, fortified with bastions, to shelter us from the incursions of the Blackfeet, whom we daily expect to visit us."[2]

By the following summer, this chapel, rough outside, must have been, within, an undreamed-of wonder to the Indians—thanks, probably, to Father Point's talented hand. One of his charming paintings shows the church at this time, imaginatively, the wooded surroundings and the colorful, decorated interior at the same time. Inside are patterned floors, decorated panels, a painted altar and retable, great pendants of drapery hanging between spirally adorned columns, and, surmounting everything, a thrilling row of finials.[3]

When the church was finished, the Indians recalled that it stood exactly where an event took place which, Father Point says, happened after Father De Smet's first short stay among the Flatheads and before his return. A dying girl had asked one of the Catholic Iroquois to baptize her; he complied. Then, seeing a vision of the Blessed Virgin, she urged her friends to listen to the Black Robes, who would come and build a house of prayer where she was dying. One of the Jesuits, probably Father Point, painted a picture of this marvel, and an oil copy of the painting hangs in the Mission today.

Early in 1842 the Indians were put to work fencing land and planting crops, and soon the mission had some of the first cattle, driven over the mountains from the west, in what would before many years be a great cattle state. Leaving again, Father De Smet went to Europe to raise money and recruit missionaries. Among those he brought back—sailing from Antwerp, around Cape Horn, and up the Columbia, an almost eight-month voyage—was Father Antonio Ravalli, from Ferrara, Italy. This well-born, well-educated, and remarkably talented man had prepared himself for his mission by studying literature, philosophy, theology, mathematics, and the natural sciences, prudently adding medicine and surgery and apprenticing himself to an artist and a mechanic. Thus, beyond obtaining a fine classical education, Father Anthony Ravalli (as his given name was henceforth anglicized) was experienced in mechanics, medicine, and the arts, all three of which fields would prove to be of immense value in educating the Indians and taming the wild frontier. Father De Smet tells of how Father Ravalli treated the sick Indians along the way, and he was to continue to treat both Indians and whites the rest of his life. Father Ravalli was thirty-three when he came to St. Mary's in the spring of 1845, and with his all-round abilities, and his talent for creating much from nothing, he had soon helped build a water-powered flourmill with buhrstones brought from Europe, and then a sawmill, the blade and other metal parts made from wagon tires. It seems likely too that he had something to do with designing the new chapel, for the following year, 1846, when Father De Smet visited the mission, he was delighted to find

> the little log church, we built five years ago, about to be replaced by another which will bear comparison with those in civilized countries, materials, everything ready to commence erecting it, the moment they can procure some ropes to place the heavy timbers on the foundation. . . . The flour mill grinds ten or twelve bushels in a day; and the saw mill furnishes an abundant supply of planks, posts, etc., for the public and private building of the nation settled here.[4]

But the new church, planned so eagerly and so energetically started, was never built, for oddly, after an inspiring start, St. Mary's did not prosper long. In the early years of the mission the Flatheads had been intensely devout and eagerly cooperative—and invariably successful in buffalo hunts and raids against their traditional enemies, the Blackfeet. By now the Blackfeet too were anxious to share the white man's magic, and in 1846 Father Point established a mission among them. To the Flatheads this was a betrayal. Disillusioned and misled by dissolute whites who clustered around the mission, especially in winter, the Flatheads became sullen and disobedient toward the Black Robes. More and more frequently they left the mission unprotected in its perpetual danger while they hunted and fished, reverting in these absences to their old non-Christian ways. Because of recurring Blackfeet raids and scares, the Black Robes decided reluctantly to close the mission for a time and work in other areas where priests were needed urgently and might have more success. In November 1850, the Jesuits sold "all the property at St. Mary's Mission" for $250 to John Owen, who was establishing a trading post, called Fort Owen, about half a mile northeast. There was a stipulation that the fields and mill property should revert to the Jesuits if they

Fort Owen – Flathead Village – St.Mary's in 1853. Color lithograph from a drawing by John Mix Stanley. Reports of Explorations and Surveys . . . , XII-1, *Plate* XXX. *In the distance (just above the mounted Indian's head) is Fort Owen; to our left (west) are some of the buildings of the abandoned St. Mary's mission, and beyond them the cottonwoods along the banks of the Bitterroot (then St. Mary's) River. The scattered cabins are the 'Flathead Village.' Thirteen years later the new St. Mary's would be built behind us and to the right. Newberry Library.*

established another mission here by the beginning of 1852. However, it was sixteen years before they returned, and by that time, as Father Palladino reports, "little was there left of the old landmarks. With the exception of the chapel, which was found in a tolerably fair condition, and a couple of log cabins that still remained, but which had become uninhabitable, everything, so to say, had to be started anew."[5] John Owen had used parts of the flourmill and sawmill in his own larger mills, which were vital in the rapid development of the Bitterroot Valley, but no one seems to have thought to record what eventually happened to the first Catholic chapel in the Northwest, with its odd fortifications, or when it finally vanished, for no trace of it remains.

Though the Jesuits had been discouraged by Flathead backsliding, as well as frightened by recurring Blackfeet raids, they had made, in nine years, a permanent change in the Flathead way of life, and this was not lost. Because of the mission activities during the 1840's and of Fort Owen in the fifties, this locality had become a valued oasis in the mountain wilderness. It was now a place where supplies could be renewed and exchanged and tired horses rested or replaced with fresh ones, a place where a man or party might pause before continuing on into the formidably rough and still mysterious mountains. At this time the mission settlement, with its fine meadows for grazing and some of the first cultivated fields in the mountains, was known by various names:

St. Mary's, the Flathead Village, the Flathead Village of St. Mary's, or Fort Owen, for the trading post was only a few hundred yards from the abandoned mission, and the Indians appear to have built their log shacks sporadically throughout the whole area.

The Blackfeet threats which had discouraged the missionaries did not stop when they left, and in 1853 John Owen abandoned his fort and headed toward the Columbia. He never reached it, for destiny—in the person of Second Lieutenant Rufus Saxton, Fourth Artillery—turned him back. Saxton had been sent by the War Department, via Panama, to Columbia Barracks in Washington Territory, there to organize a supply train and proceed to establish a provision depot at "the Flathead village of St. Mary's," after which he was to continue to Fort Benton on the Missouri. Crossing the Spokane River on 6 August 1853, Saxton

> met Mr. Owen, who, with his brother, had spent several years at St. Mary's valley, engaged in raising stock and trading with the Indians. They have at length abandoned the place, deeming it unsafe to remain longer on account of the Blackfeet Indians. They are encamped about fifteen miles from us, with all their stock, on their way to Oregon, having left their goods and other property to the mercy of the Indians. Our coming will enable them to return and re-establish their trading-post.[6]

Three weeks later, on 28 August, having arrived at "St. Mary's village," Lt. Saxton reported that

> The Flatheads have a considerable village of log-cabins around Fort Owen, and own a large number of cattle. They are now absent on a hunt across the mountains.
>
> St. Mary's is at present deserted by the priests, to whom the Indians are indebted for much of their knowledge, and many of the comforts of civilized life which they enjoy. I saw a considerable quantity of wheat, just harvested. They have also eggs, milk, potatoes, &c., articles formerly unknown to the western savage.[7]

Lt. Saxton's expedition was part of a many-pronged project. Now that the national boundaries were set in both the Southwest (1847) and the Northwest (1846), it was necessary to connect these newly American regions with the older parts of the country by means of wagon roads and railroads, for at that time the Oregon Trail, over South Pass, was the only wagon road into the entire Northwest. When, in 1853, Oregon was divided horizontally to create the new Territory of Washington, north of the Columbia and the forty-sixth parallel, the newly appointed governor, Isaac Ingalls Stevens, headed an exploratory expedition to determine the best route for a railroad between the Mississippi and the Pacific through the rough and largely unknown area near the nation's new northern boundary. Because of its location as a convenient halfway point between the Missouri and Columbia valleys, its mild climate, and its already developed advantages as a supply and wintering base, the St. Mary's Valley was an important asset to the many surveys made in 1853 and the years immediately following.

For the Flatheads, the continuing contacts with whites, and the business opportunities afforded by these bustling and peaceful military expeditions, were important civilizing influences that helped preserve what the missionaries had started. Realizing the advantages they had enjoyed with the Jesuits, the Flatheads, though visited intermittently by priests, began again to send delegations to the Black Robes, one of them to Santa Clara, California, to beg Father Gregory Mengarini, one of the original founders of St. Mary's, to come back. Finally, in 1866, the Jesuits did return. They chose a new site, on higher land, less than a mile southeast of the original complex, and here they built the present chapel, finished in 1867, and several other pine-log buildings. Father Ravalli, who had been one of the priests who left the mission when it closed in 1850, was reassigned here when it was re-established. He designed this second church, which, with one other log structure, the Pharmacy, is all that now remains of the mission buildings. Father Ravalli designed and made many of the details and furnishings of the new church, including the altar, though much of the paneling and other fine woodwork probably are the work of the skilled carpenter Brother William Claessens. He had come here in 1841 with Fathers De Smet, Point, and Mengarini, and was brought back in 1866, along with Father Ravalli, when Father Joseph Giorda, General Superior of the Missions, made the re-established St. Mary's his headquarters.

The Mission structure today is three logs long. The first two logs encompass the chapel—the pilaster-supported arch inside expresses the joint—but beyond, in the third log and under a lower roof, are two smaller rooms. Though these two rooms are connected inside by a door in their common partition, each has also its own outside entrance, so that there are two doors, side by side, in the south wall. Another door in the west end, off center, once led into another room, beyond which was still another, all being connected in a line with the chapel. The two vanished rooms (one a blacksmith shop) burned a few years after they were built, leaving the chapel aligned with the two remaining rooms, where Father Ravalli lived and worked during the last years of his life. One can still sense his presence there in the things he made and used: his desk and bookshelves—painted a fine, old red—rising against the wall and even penetrating the present ceiling, its drawers repeating the irregular octagon we will see again in the chandelier plaque on the chapel ceiling; his little table that could tilt to serve as a drawing board; a wonderful

Crucifix made by Father Ravalli, probably 1863–64. Carved wood, painted, with hinged arms for the re-enactment of Christ's Passion in Good Friday services. St. Ignatius Mission, Montana. H. A.

rocking chair, obviously made by hand and now lacking one arm; a corner cupboard, incongruously subtle in design and workmanship; a broken amphora, one of a pair, of painted and gilded wood, surely too fine not to have been made for the altar. The other amphora, somewhat less broken, is displayed currently in the little museum in the Pharmacy, which also contains an interesting, old painting of the Mission showing it with the two vanished rooms still attached. Drawn, apparently, by a local artist, it has a fascinating, homemade frame decorated with applied-relief buffalo skulls.

The Pharmacy is starkly simple. Inside, it is all one room, with a ladder-like stair rising along the east wall to a trap door near the middle. This may not be the original arrangement, since the attic floor appears to have been rebuilt about the turn of the century when the Pharmacy was used as a dwelling; one can still see where the older pole joists sat in the wall logs. There are two doors, one in the middle on the south, crowned outside with a wooden pediment, a half circle—all one board—an arresting deviation from the triangular pediments over the flanking windows. This sole ornament, valiant and pathetic, overwhelmed by the crude and sturdy log reality of the structure and the open vastness of the country, still reminds us in this mountain valley, as it must have suggested to both Indians and whites in the wilderness, that there are finer things: grace and round-arched architecture, art and the Church, Italy and Rome. The other door, toward the south corner in the east wall, is surrounded inside with cabinetwork, neatly designed and built: the storage for Father Ravalli's medicines. These cabinets, like the round pediment outside, contrast appealingly with the surrounding logs. One wonders why there were two doors so close together; perhaps this side door, like the end door in the chapel structure, once led into some long gone adjoining room or lean-to.

In front of the low, extended, log chapel and over an open vestibule, rises the gracefully sturdy, square tower, its flanking siding bravely, briefly, and ineffectually trying to hide the underlying logs, its latticed windows puzzlingly out of alignment. But the octagonal colonnade around the bell, the sheet-metal dome, and the wooden cross make an elegant and satisfying termination.

Startlingly rich, subtle, and finished compared to its rough outside, the Mission interior has a fully developed 'carpenter Gothic' style that suggests considerable familiarity with the scroll-saw, board-and-batten American architecture of its time. Entering through the plainest of recessed doors, we see, from the low space under the choir loft and past its four supporting columns, an exciting inner vista: a higher, deeper, richer, more colorful space beyond. At first there were no benches—they and their round-knobbed, varnished, tongue-and-groove fence were added years later for the whites—and the whole floor was once one open space up to the lacy altar rail, for the Indians preferred to sit and kneel on the floor. Beyond the rail, everything—the three arches, the altar, the canopy, and the two baldachins which seem to bow gracefully and reverently inward—serves to prepare us for the delicately framed niche holding the statue of the Blessed Virgin. Father Ravalli carved this image—with a pen knife, it is said, from "one block of wood." The figure, appealingly tender and gracious, has a wooden, classic simplicity, with just a hint of a baroque turn. Perhaps it is all of one piece, but the dark, horizontal line just above the knees, cutting straight across every fold in the robe, seems unexplainable except as a joint, though the advantage of two pieces so joined is puzzling. The crescent moon and the serpent under the Virgin's feet appear separate even from each other.

The insistent fascination with the idea of "one block" seems to have diverted attention from the remarkable statue of St. Ignatius under the baldachin on the right. Father Ravalli made it too. Anything but a single block, it is a fascinating collage, an amalgam of many pieces and differing materials: carved and painted wood for the head, hands, shoes, and books; glass eyes; stiffened and painted canvas for the robe (though the same romantic myth that calls the Virgin statue "one block" describes this robe as "deerhide"); a metal halo; a real belt; a real rosary; and actual printed paper pasted on the book the saint shows us. The high quality of this performance, and its professional competence, have blinded many to the fact that it is homemade. Under the circumstances we expect something quaint and crude, but this far more vital figure easily holds its own with the lovely commercial statue of a dark-skinned Mary and the Christ Child in the opposite baldachin.

There is something about the manly shape of St. Ignatius' head, and his hands, and about the way the paint is applied, that resembles another statue, almost life-size, at St. Ignatius Mission. It is a crucifix, carved and painted realistically: bloodstained, the face set in the grimace of agony surviving death. The movable arms, once supporting the tortured figure, now rest quietly at its sides in a display case. Father Ravalli made this crucifix for the old wooden church at St. Ignatius, probably when he was assigned there in 1863 and 1864, and it is still used to re-enact Christ's Passion during Good Friday services. The Most Reverend James O'Connor, Bishop of Omaha, who visited St. Ignatius in June 1877, described the church he found there as

> a much finer building than one would expect to find in such a place. It is a frame, 90 × 40 feet, with a good stone foundation, and is in the Roman style, with clere-story, columns and apse. It was designed by Father Ravalli, and built about fifteen years ago by the Indians under the superintendence of another father. It has side altars, statues and pictures, but the decorations are rather gaudy, though on that account all the better adapted to the taste of the

worshipers. A platform eight or ten feet square takes the place of the pulpit, and on it stands a wooden crucifix, carved by Father Ravalli, and of rare merit, I should say, for an amateur artist.[8]

Though the statue remains, the old, wooden church at St. Ignatius was replaced by the present brick church, built in 1891 and decorated inside with a remarkable series of paintings done in the early twentieth century by Brother Joseph Carignano.

On St. Mary's altar stand six tall, gilded candlesticks, which Father Ravalli turned from wood and set on cubes, each cube faced with a square, framed panel and resting on four spreading feet; the lips are crimped tin. Two richly painted and gilded urns probably once graced the altar; both are broken now—and retired. Though they are of wood, Father Ravalli turned, carved, painted, and gilded them so that they appear to be of gold and some precious veined marble. There is more than a hint of Italy in the sophisticated shapes and simulated materials of these classically graceful vases; their dramatically lush marbling, particularly successful, reminds one of the marbling on the wooden altars at Cataldo.

Flanking all three of the statues there are fixtures for holding sconces, but at one time the church was lighted also by the kerosene chandelier which still exists in one of the back rooms. Kerosene had begun to replace candles all over the world by the mid-1860's. In the chapel ceiling there is an octagonal plaque which must once have framed the necessary chandelier hook, gone now and its place covered by a small board. Later, there were electric lights, with frilled glass shades hanging from cords, probably installed when the benches were added, but these are used no longer, and the wires are dead.

One gets the impression at first that the whole interior is white, but part of the glowing life of this movingly beautiful room stems from the subtle impact of its varying colors. (There are differing surfaces too: planed lumber everywhere save in the battened ceiling, where the unplaned boards still show their saw marks through the paint.) The ceiling is all white, as well as the upper walls and baldachins, the round molding surrounding the altar arches, the niche frame, the four small shelves flanking it, and the confessional. A light blue subtly differentiates the walls inside the three altar arches, inside the baldachins, and inside the statue niche, appearing elsewhere only on the background parts of the canopy. A creamy white warms the conventionalized wave above the altar arches, the pendants of the canopy, the baldachin bases, the altar rail, and the altar itself with its two low stands. The floor is grey. A light tint of beige accents the structural parts: the pilasters supporting the room arch, the columns of the choir loft, the posts and base and top moldings of the loft railing, the wainscot, the moldings surrounding the three arches, the shelves above the doors at the sides of the altar, the main door, and the moldings and dentils of the canopy. The canopy monogram is gold with accenting lines of dark red; it seems to glow on a background that grades from light yellow around the letters to a medium bluish grey at the ends. The carved statue of the Virgin is, surprisingly, not monochrome, but broken areas of grey and pink. It stands on a dark green serpent, horned and eared, whose open mouth shows red, with white teeth.

Who but Father Ravalli could or would have planned and carried out this sensitive, logical design—extensive and complex, yet so subtle we do not notice it even as it moves us? The paint appears to be original, still fresh after a century in the clean Montana air.

During the sixteen years St. Mary's was closed, great changes had taken place in western Montana. Trappers took to farming and new settlers arrived, but a more rapid transformation, characteristic of many other parts of the West in the years after 1850, resulted from frequent discoveries of gold and the consequent 'rushes' that peopled and occasionally civilized some of the remotest pockets of the mountains. A succession of rich strikes in the early sixties, in the area somewhat east and southeast of the Bitterroot Valley (Gold Creek, Bannack, Virginia City, Helena), populated that region almost overnight, and made Montana a territory in 1864.

Although the mining camps boomed, the country was still raw, and there were few physicians and priests to tend the host of miners and settlers in their crises of body and soul. A hundred miles or two from the mines, Father Ravalli found himself called upon frequently to serve as physician, often far from St. Mary's, as long as he was able to move about. Returning from one of these errands, he fell sick himself and hovered near death. He recovered somewhat, but lay for four years an invalid, paralyzed from the waist down. And yet, as Father Palladino tells us, "while in this condition, almost to his dying day, he kept on doing good to all who came to him for comfort and medical assistance."[9] George G. Vest, a junketing senator from Missouri sent to investigate Indian reservations in Wyoming and Montana in 1883, reported to Congress that he had talked with Father Ravalli at St. Mary's, "and when I visited him at his little room in the mission he was lying there, having been bed-ridden for five years and still administering medicines and performing surgical operations on each recurring day."[10]

In the Pharmacy there is a stretcher which Father Ravalli built so he could be carried, in a covered spring wagon, to the sick and dying. Finally even this was too much, and, one day late in 1884, Father Ravalli died at St. Mary's. His grave, in the Indian cemetery as he wished, is aligned with the Mission, which still stands on a quiet street at the edge of Stevensville, Ravalli County, Montana.

Earlier, in 1872, the Federal Government had moved most of the Indians farther north to the Flathead Indian Reservation on the Jocko River. (A little beyond, at St. Ignatius, in the morning shadow of the Mission Range, the Jesuits had already established a mission in 1854.) But Chief Charlot refused to recognize the legality of this land exchange and with his band continued to live near St. Mary's, where his log house still stands behind the church. It was not until 1891 that this sadly reduced remnant of Flatheads finally left the Bitterroot Valley. Thereafter, the old Mission church served the local white congregation until 1954, when the new St. Mary's was built nearby. But for the addition of benches and electric lights, Old St. Mary's seems hardly to have changed since it was built, though in 1962 the century-old bottom logs, rotting on the earth, were carefully replaced with square timbers, placed this time on cement foundations. This has leveled the structure somewhat, and today the old church, because of its touching beauty and its splendid setting—and its history, which one senses without knowing—continues to attract a steady stream of visitors.

Cast-iron latch on the door to the choir loft, St. Mary's Mission. H. A.

REMEMBERING the gracefully-sawed, carpenter-Gothic woodwork which contributes so much to the character and charm of St. Mary's interior, it is puzzling to find almost irreconcilable differences, in both structure and decoration, between this and the other Mission for which Father Ravalli is famous, Cataldo. Yet these differences are not of quality but result largely from differing conditions and opportunities. Cataldo, planned twenty years earlier, rose like an exotic miracle in an almost total wilderness, where even log houses were rare; St. Mary's was built in a settled community, where logs were already old-fashioned, where mill-sawed and mill-planed lumber—even scroll-sawing—was available, and where supply trains, carrying ideas as well as baggage, arrived with something approaching regularity. Both churches, though, possess vitalities, beauties, and personalities that set them apart—and this, resulting largely from Father Ravalli's genius, unites them.

In 1842 Father Point had established a mission, dedicated to the Sacred Heart, among the Coeur d'Alene Indians. On the St. Joe River, just south of Coeur d'Alene Lake in northern Idaho, it proved to be badly located. Because of recurring floods, in 1846 the mission was moved to a hill above the Coeur d'Alene River about twenty miles east of the lake, a community later to be called Cataldo. Here a temporary chapel (made of cedar bark) served during the more urgent work of opening fields and building a mill, a barn, and other necessary structures. Father Joseph Joset, who was then at the Sacred Heart Mission, described, years later, the beginning of the present church:

> The FF. thought then (1853) they could undertake a decent church. F. Ravalli an Italian was not only a philosopher and theologian: he was a skillful physician, a painter, a sculptor; now he proved himself an architect: he drew the plan of a church 90 ft (porch included) by 40; 25 ft from floor to ceiling. How he dared such an undertaking, with the means at his command, how he succeeded, it passes my comprehension. He had but one single white man to help him Br. V. Magri, a maltese joiner. . . . All the work was to be executed by a very small tribe of savages. . . . They were counted then 320 souls. . . . Large quantity of heavy timbers were to be hewn, 24 post over 25 feet long, squared 2½ by 2½ feet some 3 by 3. Sills, joists, wall plates, rafters, all in proportion; 20,000 feet of boards to be manufactured at the saw-pit, to be dressed by hand, 50 thousand shingles; stones for the foundations to be dug from the mountains, 30,000 cubic feet; then the whole to be brought to place, on the top of the hill: the stones ½ mile, timbers some more than a mile; large quantity of clay to serve as mortar and filling between the posts.
>
> Trucks with block wheels were roughly made and for want of sufficient teams were drawn mostly by hands.
>
> They gathered from the prairies a sufficient quantity of fibres to make all the ropes needed, and made all other preparations for they were left entirely to their own industry.
>
> Please remark that no pay of any kind was given; the only thing they received was a portion of poor mush once a day: (the only grumbling was against the cook, because in his dividing it, too much of the thick stuff adhered to his big spoon).
>
> The writer happened to pass there while the work was beginning: the place looked like a large bee hive: men, women children all were busy: some at the saw-pit; others making mortises, tenons or shaping columns; some again carrying water, or mixing the clay, which others used as mortar in walling the foundations, and Magri having an eye to every thing. . . .
>
> Came the raising of that ponderous frame: think of savages putting up those massive posts, elevating 30 feet from the ground beams of 80 feet hewn 2 by one foot: the whole was executed without any serious accident. The roof was made water proof, but unhappily not snow-proof: thence every spring the snow driven in by wind melted and caused an inundation, by which both ceiling and floor were spoiled, as it can be seen today.
>
> Much work remained yet to be done: the filling between the posts, all round, the flooring and ceiling; then the boarding outside and inside; but not all at once; there was no question of saw mills, much less of planing mills: all the cutting, dressing of lumber, the engrooving was to be done by hands, altogether new to this kind of labor. Of course it should be done at intervals; the indians had to provide for their living, which at that time was done by hunting, fishing and root digging; for the Mission's farm could not feed them all the year round; besides the people, on account of old habits could not be kept stationary; it would have killed them; so the work had to be resumed when they gathered at the Mission for religious instruction for which they have always shown great eagerness.
>
> To fill between the posts two ways were obvious: either hewn logs or adobes: both seemed to take too much time and labor: another way, rather novel, was adopted. Two rows of poles were fastened between the posts like two wide parallel ladders and on them the window frames: then large ropes of straw, well soaked with wet clay, were woven on them from top to bottom, making like a double wall, the space between filled afterwards: an advantage of this kind of work was that all hands could be utilized.
>
> Meanwhile the boys were sawing, dressing, engrooving and placing the floor, though not without nails, as some body has published.[11]

Though Father Joset says that the decision to build was made in 1853, it must have been earlier, for by the end of that year the church was "almost finished." The preparations alone could easily have required years of the interrupted labor Father Joset describes. When Father Ravalli left St. Mary's in November 1850, he was assigned to the Sacred Heart Mission, probably to help with the new church. He is said to have arrived with only an axe, an auger, some ropes and pulleys, and a pen knife, and some people have concluded that the glorious church at Cataldo was built with only these few tools. More probably, though, by the time Father Ravalli arrived, the mission, adequately supplied with tools, had already made immense preparations according to his plans. The next spring (1851) Father Joset was sent to St. Paul's Mission at Kettle Falls, and Father Ravalli, at the Sacred Heart Mission, could himself supervise the building of its church.

Father Ravalli's plan had been splendidly simple, daring in scale yet adapted to the materials at hand. The foundation was of the local stone, which tends to break into squarish blocks, and, for want of lime, cemented with clay. On this foundation rest huge sills, squared from enormous trees, and on these stand gigantic posts, those along the sides about twenty inches square, those on the front larger. Held upright by braces, these posts support two sets of beams, one at the top and another about two-fifths of the way down—between the upper and lower windows. All these timbers are mortised together, and locked with big, wooden pegs driven into auger holes. More holes, bored into the sides of the posts only a few inches apart, support the ends of horizontal poles, which stretch from post to post making ladder-like walls between them. Each post has two sets of these ladders, one near the outer edge and one near the inner, so that when the Indians interwove twisted ropes of straw soaked in liquid clay and then plastered this over with more clay, daubed by hand, they made inner and outer adobe walls. The space between

Sacred Heart Mission on the Coeur d'Alene River. Color lithograph from a drawing by John Mix Stanley, who has shown himself drawing the scene, 13 October 1853. Reports of Explorations and Surveys . . . , XII-1, *Plate* XXXV. *Newberry Library.*

these walls, as Father Joset says, was then filled with more clay. Because of this insulation the church stays cool even on the hottest day. These adobe walls stood unprotected until, in 1865, Father Joseph Caruana covered them with clapboards outside and pine sheathing inside. The big posts, however, project beyond the sheathing inside and on the front to divide the structure into bays, and so articulate the walls visually. The steep roof is made of seven sets of rafters, about ten inches square, resting above the seven posts on each side. Notches in the rafters hold closely spaced horizontal poles, long since covered with sawmill shingles. The original cover must have been hand-split from local cedar.

In October 1853, when Governor Isaac I. Stevens of Washington Territory—which then included northern Idaho and even part of Montana—stayed two days at the Sacred Heart Mission, he found the church virtually complete. He mentioned it in his report on the Territory to the President of the United States:

> The Coeur d'Alene Indians . . . are much indebted to the good Fathers for making considerable progress in agriculture. They have abandoned polygamy, have been taught the rudiments of Christianity, and are greatly improved in morals and in the comforts of life. . . .
>
> They have a splendid church, nearly finished by the labors of the Fathers, brothers and Indians; a large barn; a horse-mill for flour; a small range of buildings for the accommodation of the priests and brothers; a storeroom; a milk or dairy-room; a cookroom, and good arrangements for their pigs and cattle. They are putting up a new range of quarters, and the Indians have some twelve comfortable log cabins. The church was designed by the superior skill of the mission, Father Ravalli, a man of skill as an architect, and undoubtedly, judging from his well-thumbed books, of various accomplishments. Father Gazzoli [the Superior] showed me his several designs for the altar, all of them characterized by good taste and harmony of proportion. The church, as a specimen of architecture, would do credit to anyone, and has been faithfully sketched by our artist, Mr. Stanley. The massive timbers supporting the altar were from larch trees five feet in diameter, and they were raised to their place by the Indians, with the aid simply of a pulley and a rope.[12]

Reporting that the Coeur d'Alene Indians had abandoned polygamy, Governor Stevens was probably making a pointed and proud comparison between his Indians and the Utah Mormons, who had begun the practice openly only the year before. The artist ("Mr. Stanley") was John Mix Stanley, an important recorder of the early West. He was already famous for his Indian portraits and scenes of Indian life, painted in many parts of the country, including the Southwest and Oregon, when he was appointed artist on the government-sponsored expedition, led by Governor Stevens, to determine the best route for a railroad from the Mississippi to the Pacific. His lithograph of the mission buildings in the official *Reports* shows them from the northwest, the church outwardly complete, across the bend in the river and against the wooded mountains—still the best view.

Since there are no "massive timbers supporting the altar," and no need for any, it seems likely that Governor Stevens, impressed enough by their size to mention them in more than one account, meant the two great posts on either side of the altar and supporting not it but the arch and vault above it. The exceptional bulk of these posts results from their position, which requires that they be seen from three sides, whereas the wall posts are seen from only one. To give the effect of pilaster-like projections matching those of the wall posts, but in three directions, these posts have a cross-shaped section, each arm of the cross being the same size and shape as the projecting parts of the square wall posts. When Governor Stevens saw these "massive timbers," they were newly erected and probably still bare, so that their magnitude was striking. Today, we see them covered with aging fabrics (white muslin with printed calico borders), spread over the huge blocks long ago, and obscuring the fact that the wood beneath is all of one piece. Only high up, just below the springing of the arch and just above the frieze-like capital (with its white-on-red, sawed relief of grapes and wheat), can one still see small strips of the big posts where they are yet bare, and realize that each of these clustered piers is one tree and measures up to Father Joset's "3 by 3" feet.

Other exceptionally large timbers in the structure are the six posts across the front, which stand like pilasters behind the six columns of the portico. While most of the wall posts project only on the interior, these were designed to project both inward and outward, the two corner posts extending beyond both the front and side walls. Outside, these pilasters are twenty-eight inches across. Much shorter, the dies in the column pedestals are equally thick.

Though Governor Stevens described the mission church as "nearly finished," he noted in his diary the day he left, 15 October 1853: "We started at 8 o'clock, after having given brother Charles as many lariet ropes for raising the timbers of the church as we could spare."[13] Five years later, when Father De Smet stayed at the Sacred Heart Mission between November 1858 and February 1859, he described it as possessing

> a handsome church, which would be a credit to any civilized country. It is ninety feet in length by thirty-five in width and thirty in height, with a portico supported by six massive columns. There are three altars, adorned with three magnificent pictures, brought from Rome. The beautiful statues of the holy Virgin and of Saint John at the foot of the cross, artistically sculptured by Father Ravalli, Coeur d'Alene missionary, attract especial attention. . . .
>
> The redskins are fond of work. "The construction of their handsome church," said Father Gazzoli, "was the most agreeable pastime for them." All their leisure time they devoted to transporting the stones and timbers necessary in the construction. "To forbid a Coeur d'Alene to take part in the work, or to drive him away, is a very severe punishment for him."[14]

In 1857 Father Ravalli was sent to Colville, and the same year Father Joset returned to the Sacred Heart Mission. In 1859, reporting on mission activities, Father Joset wrote:

> No one sees our church without testifying his astonishment. It is entirely the work of the Indians, except the altars. It is a magnificent monument to the faith of the Coeur-d'Alênes, who have given the lie to their name by its erection. If it were finished, it would be a handsome

church even in Europe. The design is by Father Ravalli. It is 90 feet long by 40 wide. It has 28 pillars, $2\frac{1}{2}$ feet square by 25 feet in height. All the rest is of timber, and in proportion. It was all cut, raised, and roofed by the savages, under the direction of a Father; they also filled it in, and built the foundation-walls, which are from two to five feet high, and of proportionate thickness. The Indians brought the stones from a distance of eight hundred feet, did all the mason work, and would accept no recompense. It is a great grief to us that we cannot finish it. There are two fine altars, with handsome pictures of the Sacred Heart and of the Blessed Virgin, but all the rest is naked, without doors, windows, or flooring, and not being framed in on the outside, I fear it will rot before it is completed. The neophytes have done their best: but in the absence of resources, we cannot continue the work.[15]

It would be another six years before Father Caruana sheathed the walls, but, though the work went slowly because the Indians still found it necessary to leave frequently to hunt, fish, and dig camass roots, the delays themselves had one good result. A generation was growing up that looked on the Mission as its home, and more and more Indians built their log huts nearby and began to cultivate land. As the Fathers had always hoped, the Coeur d'Alenes had an aptitude for farming and, finding that those who farmed always had plenty of food, while those who only hunted faced recurring starvation, the young mission-trained Indian men all cultivated fields. Thus the Coeur d'Alenes gradually gave up their old roving ways. Their last hunt was in 1876, and the following year, when the Federal Government set the boundaries of the Coeur d'Alene Indian Reservation somewhat to the southwest, many of the Indians were already farming on the prairies there.

Since the Old Mission (as it came to be called) was not included in this reserve, the Indians had to leave behind the great church they had toiled so long to build, and which Father Joset called perceptively "probably the most remarkable building in all Idaho."[16] Moved to the Reservation, the mission activities centered in a new village, named Desmet, and the Old Mission was used only intermittently. For a decade Father Joseph M. Cataldo made it his headquarters after he was made Superior of all the Rocky Mountain Missions in 1877—the year the Indians left. Father Cataldo had come among the Coeur d'Alenes in 1865; the little town of Cataldo, Idaho, about a mile above the Old Mission, and originally a station on the Union Pacific Railroad, was named for him. Perhaps for this reason, and because the name Cataldo is shorter and more easily said—and because it suggests better the quaint, exotic character of the Old Mission—no one ever calls the Coeur d'Alene Mission of the Sacred Heart by its true name.

After the mission was abandoned, the outbuildings gradually disappeared, and the church itself began to fall into ruin. But there has always been some odd magic about this quaint chapel, this classic anachronism of the frontier, which intrigues men's minds and hearts and will not let them forget it. Some works of art seem to possess this quality, an appeal which survives disaster, ruin—even restoration. We can be grateful that in the late 1920's, long before 'historic preservation' and 'the American heritage' were household phrases—or even generally respectable—citizens of the surrounding country, both in Idaho and Washington, worked together to repair the old structure and preserve it as a historic monument.

In 1924 the Jesuits had deeded the property to the Diocese of Boise, and early in 1925, Bishop Gorman of Boise appointed a committee to plan the restoration of the Old Mission. Many people of the area responded. In September 1926 the cities of Coeur d'Alene, Wallace, Kellogg, Burke, and Mullan, Idaho, cooperating with the Spokane Chamber of Commerce, organized an automobile pilgrimage to the Old Mission. Of the two thousand visitors, many were Coeur d'Alene Indians. At a High Mass a choir of Indians from Desmet sang the responses in Latin and Father Cataldo, then ninety, spoke to the Indians in their own tongue. Now every year, on 15 August, the Indians still come for a special service in the Old Mission.

In 1927, the Knights of Columbus of Idaho provided funds for a new roof and for repairing the supports of the portico. When Bishop Edward J. Kelly, who succeeded Bishop Gorman in 1928, enthusiastically approved the plans, already made locally, to restore the Old Mission thoroughly, action followed. The Kiwanis Club and Chamber of Commerce of Kellogg, the Board of Trade of Wallace, the Chambers of Commerce of Coeur d'Alene and Spokane, and the Knights of Columbus of Idaho, as well as committees in Lewiston, Moscow, and Orofino, collected money for the restoration. The Associated Mining Companies of the Coeur d'Alenes gave $5,000 of the nearly $12,000 collected.

This money was used to repair the foundation (replacing some of the clay with cement); to level, strengthen, and renew the floors (which are original only around the altar); to cover the outer walls with new sheathing; to align the portico columns; to repair the façade; to make new steps from large logs; to renew details of the interior; and to paint the whole exterior white. Thanks to this rescue work—done in time—the church still stands in good condition.

Today there are still few roads in this part of Idaho, which is so rough that it attracts only miners, lumbermen, a few ranchers cramped in the minute valleys, and tourists. One of these few roads, the second wagon road to cross Idaho (the first was the Oregon Trail, far to the south), passed the Mission while it was still being built. A military road connecting Fort Benton at the head of the navigable Missouri with Fort Walla Walla on the Columbia, it was surveyed and built

HISTORIC "OLD MISSION" CHURCH NEAR CATALDO.

Reproduction of a photograph showing the Sacred Heart Mission with four urns on the gable. C. J. Brosnan, History of the State of Idaho *(Charles Scribner's Sons, 1918), page 79.*

with all but incredible labor and difficulty between 1856 and 1862 under the direction of Captain John Mullan. While constructing adjacent parts of what came to be called the 'Mullan Road,' he and his crew camped at the mission in 1858 and called it "a St. Bernard in the Coeur d'Alène Mountains."[17] During the 1960's an expressway (Interstate 90) began to supersede the older road, sweeping through the already crowded mining towns in the narrow canyon. When this throughway was finished locally, late in 1966, a huge sign of the traditional white on green announced an exit where one might stop to see the CATALDO MISSION – NATIONAL HISTORIC LANDMARK. Passing tourists, perplexed, see a huge, white barn on a hilltop, but an odd splendor in the façade attracts some and makes them stop.

Closer inspection does not diminish the wonder. Incredible in these mountains, the pediment with its sunburst is a perfect and fascinating amalgam of Roman Jesuit architecture and mid-nineteenth-century, boom-town American building. Disdaining the roof line, the false-front gable describes contrapuntal angles and curves, suddenly steadied by a pair of stately urns. Generations of Idaho school children puzzled at this odd contour and ornament in a crude but alluring reproduction of the church in their "Idaho History" book. There were four urns on the gable when that photograph was taken (some time before 1918); a pair, now vanished, stood on the upper steps, flanking the arch. The two surviving urns, slightly larger, call to mind the two statues still inside the church, and the statue of the Flathead Virgin, all cut from wooden blocks by Father Ravalli's talented hand.

The six columns of the portico rise with an impressive, classic precision, deliciously tempered by their handmade imperfections—and a century and a quarter of weathering that has given the old, once neglected wood a texture as appealing as veined marble. Above the door, a glass transom—one sheet, vast for its time and place—no longer astonishes in an age of glass. In its center another marvel of nineteenth-century skill goes equally unappreciated: Father Ravalli's tour-de-force depiction of the Sacred Heart, painted on the back of the glass—finishing touches first and background last.

Bedside Stand. Pine, painted green.
(opposite) Prie-dieu. Pine, painted green, with green velvet upholstery. Both made by Father Ravalli in 1870 for the McCormick family of Missoula, Montana. Archives of the Oregon Province of the Society of Jesus, Gonzaga University.

Entering through the wide-paneled, green doors, many people, unprepared by the gable, the colonnade, and the transom, gasp in astonishment. The interior is another world: calm, clear, classic, a startling, remote island of old European tradition and logic. Yet the finish is of the frontier, engagingly crude, with an overwhelming vitality and a look of incredible antiquity.

Once open and clear for the Indians, the floor is clogged now with lumber benches. The walls, surprisingly high, have turned the wonderful brown that bare pine achieves when it is left alone for something over a century. They are alive with the fascinating, disconcerting rhythms of varying widths and lengths of hand-planed boards that make up the panels surrounding the windows. This subtle yet vitally varying pattern is held in check by the precise edge moldings, the massive bass repeats of the huge post-pilasters—painted a dull slate—and the horizontal beams (both posts and beams project beyond the wall plane). The wide ceiling panels, recessed beyond their molded beams, are decorated with applied relief, sawed out and nailed on; each group of three varies from its similar neighbors, and each subtly is more intricate than its neighbor as they approach the apse. Their ancient paint, a gamut of fading blues, reflects light from the small-paned windows. These panels are the work of Brother Francis Huybrechts, but no doubt are from Father Ravalli's designs. Huybrechts, one of the men who had accompanied Father Ravalli on the voyage to Oregon in 1844, made also the picture frames for the stations of the cross.

The spatial rhythms created in the walls and ceiling modestly anticipate the spectacularly varying depths and heights in the apse wall: two recessed altars flanking the main one, which is set back under a higher, wooden barrel vault and half dome, ceiled with thin pine boards painted a marvelous, aging blue. These geometric hollows are enhanced by friezes, moldings, and stripes of color. It is color that we are most aware of. Like the spatial design, the color climaxes in the altar wall: soft roses and blues, deep reds and blues, an ochre band, yellow fretwork, the simulated gold of patterned fabrics and of gilded carving and metal, stenciled frame designs, illusionistic paintings, framed lithographs, wooden altars shaped and painted to imitate marble, and doors and trim of varying greens. And, flanking the arch, are two touches of dull white where Father Ravalli's carved wood statues of the Blessed Virgin and John the Evangelist stand on wonderful brackets.

One flaw mars the splendor; at the right of the entrance a corner of the interior has been walled off to shelter an old chapel. It is a gem of antiquely shaped and painted wood: an altar, baldachins, pedestals, pilasters, ceiling bosses, rich moldings and relief panels—all enhanced and articulated by a fine harmony of prodigal but controlled, marbleized color, which time has made more beautiful. This was the private chapel of the Jesuits, and Father Ravalli designed, built, and painted it in a frame structure which formerly adjoined the parsonage on the east (now the caretaker's house). Beneath this old chapel was a crypt in which several of the early Fathers were buried, but, when the deteriorating building was demolished in the early 1950's, the bodies were moved to Spokane. The chapel, too good not to save, was taken apart and somewhat reassembled inside the Old Mission; combining the two attractions seemed to offer the advantages of compactness and convenience for sightseers and for the caretaker. One cannot help thinking that the decision to move this beautiful room was a disaster, a violation of history, art, Father Ravalli's reputation, the Old Mission, and the modern pilgrim, because this architectural jewel was noticeably altered, diminished, and rearranged in transit. Yet, the chapel is still movingly beautiful, apparently indestructible; its very fragments live. This sheltered simulacrum shelters in turn an old, factory-made organ, donated by General Sherman's wife, Ellen, who, though she never visited the Mission, was long engrossed in Catholic charities.

Outside, from the river, the Old Mission looks much as it must have a hundred years ago and more. Cows still graze the slope, and tourists park their campers where Indian tepees used to stand. Ignoring the noisy highway, an osprey flies home with another branch for an already topheavy nest in a dead tree. And the river, silted up now with mine tailings but still heartbreakingly lovely, reflects the Mission, dreaming on the hill.

HOW long can they last, these aging, wooden churches, the by-products of a man who had chosen a calling greater than architecture: Cataldo with its grass-and-adobe filling and fragile paintings, St. Mary's in its weathered logs? Both churches are well used, if largely only by sightseers, and continual use, for old buildings, is their surest guarantee of survival. We can hope—and try to ensure—that both these unique and irreplaceable structures, so oddly connected with great events in our history, and protected so long by isolation and their own beauties, can far outlive our present generation, and so stand for a long time, to amuse tourists' children, and to remind us of a fabulous past and teach us that grace can rise and endure in rough surroundings. Beyond all this, though, the sheer beauty of Father Ravalli's Missions, poignantly surviving from a better world, is reason enough to treasure them, and fortunate is the man who has seen either.

Skull and crossbones. Wood, carved and painted by Father Ravalli. About half life-size. Montana Historical Society. H. A.

NOTES

[1] De Smet to Reverend and Dear Father Provincial, St. Mary's, Dec. 30, 1841, quoted in Chittenden, I, 331–34.
[2] *Ibid.*, 338.
[3] Point, 54.
[4] De Smet, *Oregon Missions*, 288–89.
[5] Palladino, 54.
[6] *Reports of Explorations and Surveys*, XII–I, 257.
[7] *Ibid.*, 261.
[8] Most Rev. James O'Connor, "The Flathead Indians," *Records of the American Catholic Historical Society of Philadelphia*, III, (1888–91), 94.
[9] Palladino, 58.
[10] *Congressional Record*, 48th C., 1st S., XV–4 (1884), 4067.
[11] Joseph Joset, S.J., "The old Coeurs d'alene Mission and its Church," 4–8, Joset MSS., Archives of the Oregon Province of the Society of Jesus, Gonzaga University, Spokane, Washington.
[12] Message of the President of the United States to Congress, 1854–55, 416, quoted in Chittenden, IV, 1274.
[13] *Reports of Explorations and Surveys*, I, 367.
[14] De Smet (The Oregon Expedition of 1858–59), *Précis Historiques*, IV, quoted in Chittenden, II, 760.
[15] Joset to Father Fouillot, Sacred Heart Mission, 21 June 1859, in De Smet, *New Indian Sketches*, 66.
[16] Joseph Joset, S.J., "Old Mission Church," 4, Joset MSS., Archives of the Oregon Province of the Society of Jesus, Gonzaga University, Spokane, Washington.
[17] Chittenden, III, 800.

BIBLIOGRAPHY

William N. Bischoff, S.J., *The Jesuits in Old Oregon, 1840–1940*, Caldwell, Idaho: The Caxton Printers, Ltd., 1945.

C. J. Brosnan, *History of the State of Idaho*, New York, Chicago, Boston: Charles Scribner's Sons, 1918.

Hiram M. Chittenden and Alfred T. Richardson, *Life, Letters and Travels of Father Pierre-Jean De Smet, S.J., 1801–1873*, 4 vols., New York: Francis P. Harper, 1905.

Rev. Edmund R. Cody, *History of the Coeur d'Alene Mission of The Sacred Heart*, Caldwell, Idaho: The Caxton Printers, Ltd., Edmund R. Cody, 1930.

William L. Davis, S.J., *A History of St. Ignatius Mission*, Spokane, Washington: C. W. Hill Printing Co., W. L. Davis, 1954.

Bernard DeVoto, *The Year of Decision, 1846*, Boston: Little, Brown and Co., 1943.

———, *Across the Wide Missouri*, illustrated with paintings by Alfred Jacob Miller, Charles Bodmer and George Catlin, with an account of the discovery of the Miller Collection by Mae Reed Porter, Boston: Houghton Mifflin Co., 1947.

John C. Ewers, *George Catlin, Painter of Indians and the West*, annual report of the Smithsonian Institution for 1955, pp. 483–528, with 20 plates, Washington, D.C.: United States Government Printing Office, 1956.

———, *Artists of the Old West*, Garden City, New York: Doubleday & Co., 1965.

Rev. Martin Florian, *The Story of St. Mary's Mission*, rev. ed., Stevensville, Montana, 1965.

Helen Addison Howard, "Padre Ravalli: Versatile Missionary," *The Historical Bulletin*, Vol. XVIII, No. 2 (January 1940), pp. 33–35.

Joseph Joset, S.J., "The old Coeurs d'alene Mission and its Church," Joset MSS., Archives of the Oregon Province of the Society of Jesus, Crosby Library, Gonzaga University, Spokane, Washington.

I. M. Leo, "Father Ravalli—Missionary, Pioneer, Teacher," *Winston's Weekly*, reprinted in *The Daily Missoulian*, Missoula, Montana, Tuesday, March 8, 1904, p. 7. (Clipping, Ravalli file, Historical Society of Montana Library.)

Lawrence B. Palladino, S.J., *Indian and White in the Northwest*, Baltimore: [J. Murphy], 1895.

Nicholas Point, S.J., *Wilderness Kingdom, Indian Life in the Rocky Mountains: 1840–1847*, the journals & painting of Nicholas Point, S.J., translated and introduced by Joseph P. Donnelly, S.J., with an appreciation by John C. Ewers, New York, Chicago, San Francisco: Holt, Rinehart and Winston, 1967.

Reports of Explorations and Surveys, to ascertain the most practicable and economical route for a railroad from the Mississippi River to the Pacific Ocean. Made under the direction of the Secretary of War in 1853–4, according to acts of Congress of March 3, 1853, May 31, 1854, and August 5, 1854. 12 vols. in 13 (General Report, Vol. XII, Part I). Washington, D.C.: 1855–60.

Wilfred P. Schoenberg, S.J., *Jesuits in Montana, 1840–1960*, Portland, Oregon: The Oregon-Jesuit, 1960.

Pierre-Jean De Smet, S.J., *Letters and Sketches*: with a narrative of a year's residence among the Indian tribes, Philadelphia: M. Fithian, 1843.

———, *New Indian Sketches*, New York: D. & J. Sadlier & Co., [1865?].

———, *Oregon Missions and Travels over the Rocky Mountains, in 1845–46*, New York: Edward Dunigan, 1847.

Welcome to the Mission, Coeur d'Alene Mission of the Sacred Heart, information brochure available at the church, n.d.

FATHER RAVALLI'S MISSIONS

ST. MARY'S

St. Mary's Mission; the chapel, and Father Ravalli's living quarters from the southeast, Stevensville, Montana.

The chapel and Father Ravalli's living quarters from the northwest.

The east window in the south wall of the chapel.

The bell tower.

St. Mary's interior from under the choir loft.

The interior, showing the pilaster-supported arch marking the joint between the two sections of the log building. In the ceiling is the plaque for the chandelier fixture.

The altar wall.

The dark-skinned statue of the Blessed Virgin and the Christ Child standing in the left baldachin.

Father Ravalli's statue of St. Ignatius in the right baldachin and the painting of the appearance of the Blessed Virgin to the dying Indian girl.

The statue of St. Ignatius made by Father Ravalli.

HAERESES

A closer view.

IHS

The altar, the wooden statue of the Blessed Virgin, and the canopy.

The altar, made by Father Ravalli, with the six gilded wooden candlesticks. The crayon portrait of Father Ravalli appears to have been drawn from a photograph.

The wooden statue of the Blessed Virgin carved by Father Ravalli. When this photograph was taken (1968) the crescent moon, which should have been under the Virgin's feet with the serpent, had been removed temporarily.

The canopy over the altar.

Looking from the altar toward the entrance and choir loft.

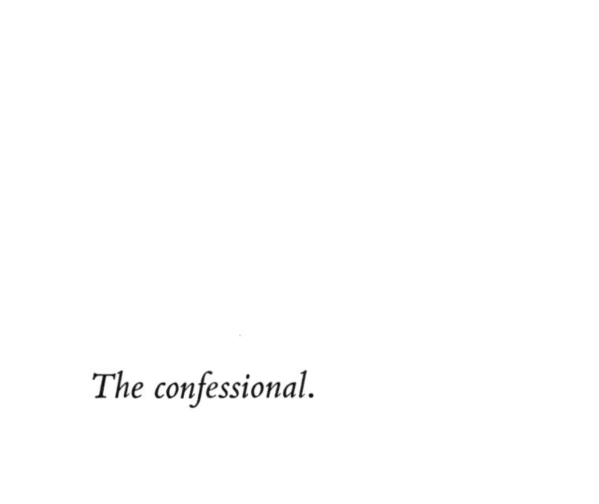

The confessional.

The west door and window of Father Ravalli's living quarters.

Father Ravalli's desk, bookcase, and rocking chair in his living quarters behind the chapel.

OFFERINGS
FOR
UPKEEP OF
MISSION

A wooden amphora (one of a pair), turned, carved, and painted by Father Ravalli to imitate gold and marble.

The Pharmacy and the chapel from the northwest.

The Pharmacy from the south.

A painting in the Pharmacy showing St. Mary's chapel with two additional log rooms attached beyond Father Ravalli's living quarters. Signed "T. C. FARLIN 1915."

Father Ravalli's stretcher in the Pharmacy.

Father Ravalli's grave and monument.

S. J.
FATHER RAVAL

CATALDO

The Coeur d'Alene Mission of the Sacred Heart from the northwest across a bend in the Coeur d'Alene River, Cataldo, Idaho.

The Sacred Heart Mission from the northwest, with the caretaker's house, formerly the parsonage (built 1868), beyond.

The Sacred Heart Mission from the southeast.

The false-front gable from behind.

The Sacred Heart Mission from the northeast.

IHS

The base of the west column of the portico (looking north from the porch).

The main door, with the Sacred Heart painted by Father Ravalli on the back of the transom glass.

The interior, looking toward the altar.

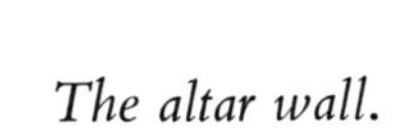

The altar wall.

The main altar.

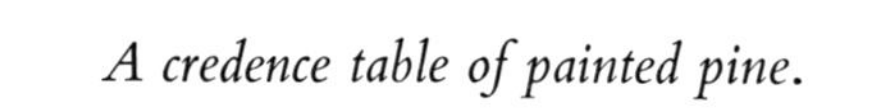

A credence table of painted pine.

The left altar. On the pier is Father Ravalli's wooden statue of the Blessed Virgin above a lithograph of St. Ignatius Loyola.

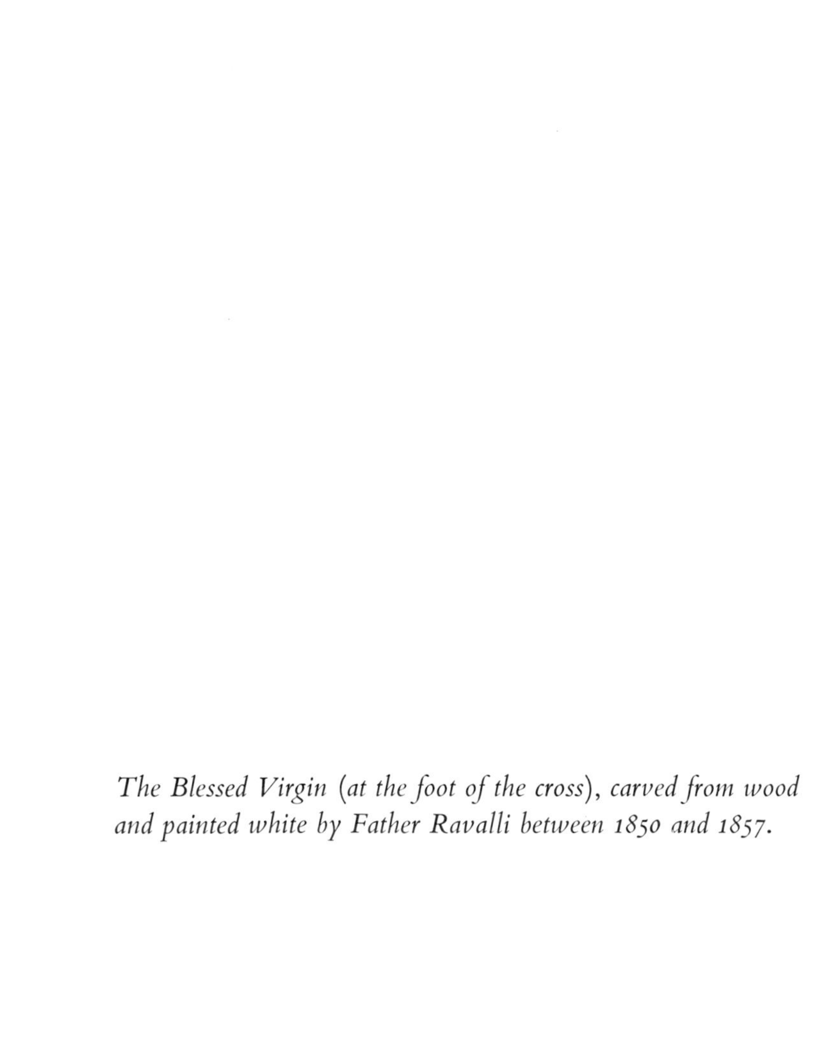

The Blessed Virgin (at the foot of the cross), carved from wood and painted white by Father Ravalli between 1850 and 1857.

St. John the Evangelist, carved from wood and painted white by Father Ravalli between 1850 and 1857.

The right altar. On the pier is Father Ravalli's wooden statue of St. John above a lithograph of St. Francis Xavier.

Putto head below the bracket supporting the statue of St. John. Carved wood, painted realistically.

The four ceiling panels.

Picture frame for a station of the cross, made by Brother Francis Huybrechts.

VIII
STATION
JÉSUS

The north wall of the west sacristy, showing clay-soaked straw woven around horizontal poles between two posts (that on the left in the outside wall and that on the right in the middle of the sanctuary wall west of the altar).

Looking north above the ceiling of the east sacristy, and showing the fifth and sixth of the seven posts in the east wall, the beams and rafters resting on them, and the pole-straw-adobe walls they support. The dark area to the right of the post on the left is the back of the painting above the left (east) altar, which is between the fifth and sixth posts.

The 'reconstructed' private chapel of the Jesuits, brought from the now-demolished frame structure where it was built originally, and installed now in the northwest corner of the Mission interior. Father Ravalli designed, made, and painted it, no doubt when he was stationed here between 1850 and 1857. Although the various parts and details are in good condition, their original relationships have been altered, and the painting above the altar was already hanging in the church before the chapel was rebuilt around it. The two columns, imitating those of the portico, are part of the reconstruction, not of the original chapel, and were made by Jerry Wilson of nearby Pinehurst, one of the men who moved the chapel here.

The gable at sunset and moonrise.

Harold Allen was born in Oregon but grew up in Idaho. He worked on ranches there and in Jackson Hole and on the Green River in Wyoming before going to Chicago to attend the School of the Art Institute of Chicago. He first studied photography there in 1938, and as an Army Air Force photographer in World War II began to photograph architecture: the cathedrals of England and the palaces of Versailles and Fontainebleau. At the University of Chicago after the war he developed his interest in architectural history and has become one of the foremost authorities in the little-cultivated field of Egyptian-Revival architecture in America. In 1964 and 1965 he was official photographer for the Chicago Project of the Historic American Buildings Survey. He began teaching photography at the School of the Art Institute of Chicago in 1948 and is now the Frederick Latimer Wells Professor there.

The plates, and those photographs identified H. A., are the work of the author.

The photographs of Cataldo Mission were taken 14 August 1967 and 8–10 July 1971, those of St. Mary's 10 August 1967, 6 August 1968, and 12–13 July 1971. All were taken with a 4″×5″ Linhof Technika camera, using four lenses: 90 mm., 150 mm., 7 in., 360 mm.

Composed in Bembo types by The Stinehour Press, Lunenburg, Vermont. Caslon titling. Printed by The Meriden Gravure Company, Meriden, Connecticut.